WEST CLIFF STORY

The Life & Times of Clacton-on-Sea's
West Cliff Theatre
1894-2008

by
NORMAN JACOBS

Celebrating the 80th anniversary of the building
of the West Cliff Gardens Concert Pavilion
and 21 years of
The Friends of the West Cliff Theatre

The Friends of the West Cliff Theatre 2008

This edition first published 2008
by The Friends of the West Cliff Theatre
Tower Road, Clacton-on-Sea,
Essex, CO15 1LE

British Library Cataloguing in Publication Data.
A catalogue record for this book is available from the British Library.
ISBN 978 09524173 1 6

Typesetting and origination by David Clark, Holland-on-Sea, Essex
Printed by Jennerprint, Tiptree, Essex

Introduction and Acknowledgements

A lot has happened since West Cliff Story was first published 14 years ago in 1994. For example, the freehold of the theatre has been bought by the West Cliff (Tendring) Trust Ltd from Tendring District Council and Francis Golightly no longer produces the Summer Show.

Although there has now been entertainment on the present site for 109 years, the current building itself is celebrating its 80th birthday this year. As this coincided with the Friends of the West Cliff's 21st anniversary, they have decided to commission an updated version of the book reflecting the changes that have taken place in those last 14 years. This new edition of West Cliff Story therefore is an attempt to bring the story up to date.

Those of us involved with the West Cliff, Friends, Trustees, staff (both voluntary and full-time), performers and patrons should be proud of what this theatre has achieved over the years and even more proud of the fact that today, more than ever, the West Cliff Theatre stands at the heart of the Tendring community, providing not just entertainment on its stage but also facilities for all manner of local clubs, societies, schools and events.

The West Cliff Theatre has a proud tradition. Long may it continue!

The author would like to thank the following for their help and support in the production of this book:

David Clark for the design and production, Ellie Clark for retyping the original book, Bridget Bentley for allowing me to reprint photographs from her personal collection, Mike Bareham and Linda Jacobs for additional photography, Mike Freeman for additional information and, of course, the Friends of the West Cliff for making the whole thing possible in the first place.

Foreword by Jimmy Cricket

"I headed for the West Cliff — what an atmosphere"

My friendship with the West Cliff Theatre goes back just over 40 years. I was a fresh faced 22 year old, straight off the boat from Ireland and I'd landed a job as a Redcoat in the Butlins Holiday Camp in Clacton.

In those days each camp housed a custom built theatre with a 3000 seat auditorium. Each Thursday they held the Redcoat gang show where the budding stars of the future would strut their stuff. But this was no X Factor. No, we knew most of the audience by their first names having mixed with them through the week, so they applauded and cheered every corny gag and off key note. At the end of the season you left the camp ten feet tall.

Being a Butlin Redcoat enabled you to get a complimentary ticket to see the other theatre shows in town. So on my first day off I headed for the West Cliff. What an atmosphere. It was 1967 so the show had Don Maclean topping with Harry Dickman as second comic. Don as we all know went on the play a big part in the sucess of the West Cliff. But there was big competition that year.

Over at the Pier's Ocean Theatre, comedian Billy Burdon (a firm favourite with the people of Clacton) was headlining his own summer show. Billy played a country yokel from Dorset and his droll deadpan delivery had the audiences rolling in the aisles). I was searching for a style then and one of the resident revue artistes in Butlins, Manny, said " Jimmy get a character. How do you think Billy Burdon gets away with that stuff he's doing over on the pier?" I didn't know then how prophetic Manny's words would turn out.

I went on to earn a crust in the crazy world of show business and in 2006 I went back to play a summer season at the West Cliff. So the wheel came full circle. During the in between period both the West Cliff and I have had our ups and downs. Along the way some really good producers have enriched the West Cliff with some fine shows. I'm thinking now of the eighties and Francis Golightly's wonderful Cascade shows, And the last couple of summers when John Warwick has put on some sparkling stuff. However to me the backbone of the West Cliff is the enthusiasm passion and commitment of the Friends of the Theatre. That and the strong management that's behind them I know will ensure the West Cliff will be still going in another 80 years.

The Green Eye of the Little Yellow God

as recited with great success by Bert Graham, founder of the West Cliff Theatre

There's a one-eyed yellow idol to the north of Khatmandu,
There's a little marble cross below the town;
There's a broken-hearted woman tends the grave of Mad Carew,
And the Yellow God forever gazes down.

He was known as "Mad Carew" by the subs at Khatmandu,
He was hotter than they felt inclined to tell;
But for all his foolish pranks, he was worshipped in the ranks,
And the Colonel's daughter smiled on him as well.

He had loved her all along, with a passion of the strong,
The fact that she loved him was plain to all.
She was nearly twenty-one and arrangements had begun
To celebrate her birthday with a ball.

He wrote to ask what present she would like from Mad Carew;
They met next day as he dismissed a squad;
And jestingly she told him then that nothing else would do
But the green eye of the little Yellow God.

On the night before the dance, Mad Carew seemed in a trance,
And they chaffed him as they puffed at their cigars;
But for once he failed to smile, and he sat alone awhile,
Then went out into the night beneath the stars.

He returned before the dawn, with his shirt and tunic torn,
And a gash across his temple dripping red;
He was patched up right away, and he slept through all the day,
And the Colonel's daughter watched beside his bed.

He woke at last and asked if they could send his tunic through;
She brought it, and he thanked her with a nod;
He bade her search the pocket saying, "That's from Mad Carew,"
And she found the little green eye of the god.

She upbraided poor Carew in the way that women do,
Though both her eyes were strangely hot and wet;
But she wouldn't take the stone and Mad Carew was left alone
With the jewel that he'd chanced his life to get.

When the ball was at its height, on that still and tropic night,
She thought of him and hastened to his room;
As she crossed the barrack square she could hear the dreamy air
Of a waltz tune softly stealing thro' the gloom.

His door was open wide, with silver moonlight shining through;
The place was wet and slipp'ry where she trod;
An ugly knife lay buried in the heart of Mad Carew,
'Twas the "Vengeance of the Little Yellow God."

There's a one-eyed yellow idol to the north of Khatmandu
There's a little marble cross below the town;
There's a broken-hearted woman tends the grave of Mad Carew,
And the Yellow God forever gazes down.

In the beginning . . .

IN 1894 Japan declared war on China; Czar Alexander III of Russia died and the infamous Dreyfus trial took place in France. In Great Britain, Queen Victoria had been on the throne for 57 years; Gladstone resigned as Prime Minister for the last time and Tower Bridge, the Blackpool Tower and the Manchester Ship Canal were all opened.

Meanwhile, closer to home in Clacton, the new Town Hall buildings (including the Operetta House, later the Savoy Theatre) were opened on the corner of Rosemary Road, High Street and Station Road; the town's fire brigade was founded and St Paul's Hall was opened in the High Street.

1894 was also the year that the 21 year old Bert Graham (real name Bert Harvey) arrived in Clacton from London to start his open air concert party. Graham had first appeared on the stage in 1890 at the age of 17. His early appearances were strictly amateur affairs as he was still a Civil Servant by profession. However in 1894 he decided to take the plunge and go into the entertainment business full time. He got together a concert party consisting of himself, his sister Lilian, Bernard Russell, Ted Honeyman and pianist Jack Devo and set out for Clacton.

There were already a number of other concert parties performing in the open air at Clacton such as L'Art Minstrels and Braide and Partridge's White Minstrels. However, Bert Graham's Concert Party was different from the ordinary Pierrot affair or the Minstrel show as he insisted that his troupe perform in evening dress at all times. The company was known as the London Concert Company and their first performances were on a patch of open ground in Agate Road.

Shows were put on at various times during the day with one evening performance under candle light. As they were completely in the open, shows had to be cancelled in bad weather. Even in good weather planks had to be placed across the then unmade roads to enable people to get to the shows. This did not however deter the crowds and it was not uncommon to have upwards of 1000 people, paying twopence a time to sit or stand on the grass listening to Bert

Messrs Graham, Russell and Bentley enjoy a quiet smoke together.

Graham's London Concert Company.

They very soon made their mark in the town and, as early as 1895, by which time the concert party had moved across Agate Road to a site on the corner of West Avenue, they were receiving notices such as these in the local paper:

- During the past week the various entertainments have been well patronised, including Bert Graham's Concert Party where a capital variety programme is given each evening. (24th July)
- Bert Graham's open-air concerts are attracting large crowds nightly. (21st August)
- Messrs Bert Graham's Company are leaving at the end of the month after a successful season. (25th September)

Before the start of the 1896 season, they were engaged to give a special performance in the new town hall in aid of the Public Clock Fund. This was given free of charge and raised the grand sum of £13 12s (£13 60p).

The programme for this one-off benefit performance gives some idea of what went into a Concert Party at the time. It began with a "highly amusing farce" called "A Kiss in the Dark", in which all the members of the Company took part. This was followed by the individual members doing their solo acts, including Lilian Graham giving a "sweet and sympathetic rendering of The Hope of Years", Florence Tench's "dramatic rendition of How we beat the Captain's Colt" and Bert Graham performing his party piece It must have been the lobster.

The finale to the show was the "ever-popular domestic comedy", The Spitalfields Weaver, again with all members of the Company (Bert and Lilian Graham, Florence Tench, Chas Freeman, Albert Sinclair and F.S. Riggs) taking part.

Graham, Russell & Bentley's Company in 1904.

Graham and Russell's Concert Party

BERNARD RUSSELL rejoined the company in time for its official start to the season at Whitsuntide and later in the year was taken into full partnership by Bert Graham, with the troupe becoming known as Graham and Russell's Concert Party.

On 27th June 1896 a significant event for the future of the West Cliff took place when the Company gave another special performance at the Town Hall. This time they were joined by several guest artistes, amongst whom was a comic singer by the name of Will Bentley. The newspaper of the time reported that "Mr Will Bentley made himself a warm favourite, all his songs being encored."

Towards the end of the 1896 season, the newspaper announced that "With the dark evenings, Messrs Graham and Russell have moved from their out-door pitch to the grand hall of Mr Badger's Riggs Retreat."

In 1897 Graham and Russell were on the move yet again, this time to the corner of Jackson Road and West Avenue where the Odeon Cinema was later to be built, a site now occupied by the Lloyd's Chemist shop and Argos. This new site did have its problems however: "Messrs Graham and Russell's Entertainments – These popular open-air entertainments, which are held in West Avenue, commenced on Monday (31st May 1897). Large numbers have flocked to the spot every evening, and the entertainments bid fair to be as enjoyable as they have been previous seasons. The only thing that has at all marred their success so far is the 'music' which proceeds from a field close by, in which swinging-boats have been erected." (Clacton Gazette 4th June 1897).

As well as performing regularly on their new site, Graham and Russell's troupe (now consisting of Bert Graham, Bernard Russell, Lilian Graham, Mr H.J. Baynton and Richard Evans) continued to perform at other venues around Clacton in special one-off concerts. They performed in a "Special Benefit Concert" at the Grosvenor Hall in Pallister Road on 24th September 1897 while on 1st October that year they

performed in the Pier Pavilion.

Bert Graham's sister, Lilian, stayed with the company for several years. She was the group's singer and was said to have had a "beautiful and melodic" voice. Though, of course, it was in the nature of concert parties that all members were expected to turn their hand to anything, comedy, singing, acting and so on. As a contemporary writer, known only as "C.B.W." said: "To sum their qualities up in a nutshell – they are artistes, to their finger tips, deservedly popular, but modest withal."

Lilian Graham

Graham, Russell and Bentley's first open air stage at the West Cliff Gardens

Advertising in the early days!

Will Bentley joins the party

According to contemporary records, Bert Graham seems to have taken a year off in 1898 and Bernard Russell took into partnership the Troupe's 1896 guest artiste, Will Bentley, on a permanent basis. The Company that year consisted of Russell and Bentley, Elsie Steadman, Will Deller, Robert Linton and Edward Britnell. The enclosure was extended and further seating accommodation was provided.

It may well have been Will Bentley who introduced a popular new turn into the show as, for the first time in Clacton, the Cinematograph was featured. According to a review of the time "The pictures comprised a variety of subjects from the Jubilee procession to a pillow fight, and were shown with remarkable clearness."

Will Bentley seems to have been at the cutting edge of new technology in the late 19th century, for, as well as being responsible for bringing the cinema to Clacton in 1898, in the year previously, he had applied to Clacton Council for permission to place a phonograph on the West Cliff! Whether this was actually on the cliff top or on the place where the West Cliff Theatre was later to be built is unfortunately not clear.

In 1899, Bert Graham rejoined the party, and it was in this year that Messrs Graham, Russell and Bentley all together in full partnership for the first time removed themselves to the Recreation Ground off Tower Road, in other words to the West Cliff Gardens and the site of the present theatre. To begin with their shows were still given in the open air. However they soon acquired a marquee to cover the stage and they also erected rows of wooden seats and a paybox. Later they enclosed the ground with a wooden fence and put a canvas roof over the auditorium – the back of which was raised three feet – and installed electric light. In hot weather the sides could be opened to let in fresh air. Altogether the make-shift hall seated 1000, while the promenade on either side permitted a similar number to enjoy the concerts.

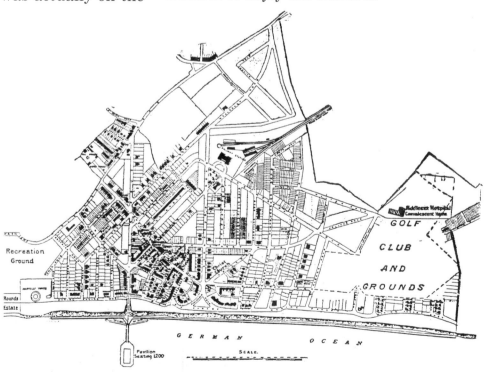

Map of Clacton-on-Sea from The East Essex Advertiser, 11th June, 1896.
The Recreation Ground that Graham, Russell & Bentley moved to is on the left.
"Pavilion Seating 1200" on the Pier is The Jolly Roger.

The Recreation Ground in 1898 before the London Concert Company's move.

Winter 1898 and the new open theatre is under construction

The new theatre open for business 1899.

A studio portrait of Messrs Graham, Russell and Bentley.

Messrs Graham, Russell and Bentley in costume during rehearsal.

Graham, Russell and Bentley each had their own speciality; Bert Graham's was the dramatic monologue and dialect song of the "countryman", Bernard Russell appears to have been something of a clown or slapstick comedian, while Will Bentley was more of the stand-up type of comic.

Map of Clacton-on-Sea from the East Essex Advertiser, 11th July 1896. The recreation Ground that Graham, Russell & Bentley moved to is on the left. "Pavilion Seating 1200" on the Pier is The Jolly Roger.

Graham, Russell and Bentley's concert party remained popular throughout the Edwardian period, or as the Clacton News put it: "Our friends Graham, Russell and Bentley keep up their old popularity. The evenings lately have been decidedly chilly, yet it is astonishing to find so many people at their outdoor concert. But it is no wonder they come. The entertainment is a good one, full of fun and merriment." Prices at this period were 1s (5p) for reserved seats, 6d and 4d for other seats and 2d to promenade.

To help boost the mid-week audiences, Graham, Russell and Bentley introduced special nights once a week. On Wednesdays there was Carnival night, when the Gardens were festooned with streamers and other similar items to liven up the proceedings, while on Mondays, it was "Lucky Programme Night", with prizes given to the lucky winners. These innovations lasted until well after the first world war.

As well as the regular company, Graham, Russell and Bentley employed guest artistes during the season. For example in 1906, Mr Kit Keen "of the London Pavilion, coon comedian and bone soloist" appeared as did Mr Harrison Walker a "baritone from the Queen's Hall in London."

Tragedy struck the company in 1910, when, after a long illness, Bernard Russell died at his parents home in Camden Town, London, at the age of 34. He had been married for just two years and left a baby son only a few weeks old. Following Bernard Russell's death, Graham and Bentley continued to put on their shows under the heading of Graham and Bentley's Concert Party. From 1912 to 1914 they employed a young singer in their company billed as a "romantic baritone". His name was Stanley Holloway, later to become famous for his monologues, his starring roles in the "Ealing Comedies" and eventually to achieve international stardom for his part as Alfred Doolittle in both the stage and film versions of My Fair Lady.

During the first world war the shows continued at the West Cliff in spite of the many

The Theatre c.1902

difficulties. The doors had to be covered with curtains and every crack had to be stopped up for fear of showing a light.

After the war performances continued in the timber theatre which had replaced the old marquee. The sides were raised and flapping canvas screens were drawn across when necessary. The Pit was tiny, just about big enough to hold a piano, but nothing more and it could be approached from under the stage.

At this period, in the early 20s, programmes carried the following notice:

The Management politely request that where necessary Ladies will remove their Hats in order not to obstruct the view of those sitting behind.

A popular performer in the 1920s was a man called Hector Gordon, a Scottish entertainer, much in the mould of Harry Lauder. Whilst behind the scenes, Mr Oakey, the scene shifter, who had been with Graham and Bentley since before the first world war, had become almost as well known as the on stage stars.

West Cliff programme 5th July, 1913

From Stanley Holloway's Autobiography *Wiv a Little Bit of Luck*:

When I was but a stripling in concert party at Clacton, concerned then only with my singing, I used to stand in the wings whenever possible to watch an entertainer called Bert Graham do his stuff. The Green Eye of the Little Yellow God was one of his big specialities and I was riveted by the conviction and relish with which he wrung every ounce of drama, suspense and colour out of this corny melodramatic yarn...

Concert party is an acid test; it's useless simply being confident in your own act; you must be prepared to help out in sketches at a moment's notice and play anything from a juvenile to a decrepit old copper...

Graham & Bentley's Concert party. Stanley Holloway is on the extreme left.

It was 1913. I was playing in concert party at Clacton for Graham and Bentley (who later went into the oyster business, as gourmets around the West End will know well!) when an exuberant, confident young man breezed into town in a two-seater car. From the moment we met Leslie Henson believed in my potential career and (I) got the chance to go into Nicely Thanks! the concert party which Leslie was going to tour with around the music halls...

Leo Bentley

Will Bentley's son

"I can remember the old West Cliff Gardens before the present theatre was built. The whole building was wood and canvas, there was no brick at all. This early building had a canvas cover with sides that could be raised in warm weather and on a nice summer's evening during the interval when the flaps were up, you could hear a rustling sound all round as the leaves of the trees which surrounded the theatre gently swayed in the breeze. It was marvellous.

Because the sides were open one got a lot of free watchers outside. It was probably good for business though as anything like that attracted trade.

My outstanding memory of the theatre was pennies and ha'pennies and chocolates from the seats that people had dropped, on Sunday mornings in particular.

One amusing incident I can remember was when a performer called Nance Haines who had rushed out to change a dress got the back of her dress entangled in her knickers. She went back on stage and probably got the biggest encore you could ever wish for!

My father used to sing comic songs; two of his favourites were Sailors don't Care and The Wreck of the Hesperus. He wasn't much of a singer and the songs turned into recitations really. He didn't have a great voice, but he put a lot of expression in to his performance. The audiences used to enjoy his songs immensely. Humour was totally different in those days, nothing distasteful about it.

On the once a week Carnival Nights the cast used to come down off the stage and mix with the audience. I can remember that well. Also at the end of every performance my father

and Bert Graham used to be outside the theatre to say goodnight and shake hands with the audience.

People who came year after year used to really appreciate this gesture."

that all around the auditorium, at about two feet intervals, there hung Japanese lanterns, all of a different design and all illuminated by electric light.

I can remember when I was young going around the stalls picking up the

CLACTON'S PIONEER ENTERTAINERS.

WEST CLIFF GARDENS THEATRE

OPENED BY SIR FREDERICK RICE, M.P.

Succeeding generations — residents and visitors—having come to regard West Cliff Gardens Concert Pavilion as " part and parcel " of the holiday season will perhaps heave a gentle sigh and momentarily ruminate on the passing of time when they gaze on the luxurious building that has now taken the place of the old temporary structure, where for three decades Messrs Bert Graham and Will Bentley—the pioneers by the way of Clacton's entertainers—have amused and charmed countless thousands, and won and retained the affection and esteem of their patrons. Although a change of scene has taken place at the Gardens, we venture to think there will be no change in the relationship of proprietor and patron, which has been of a character unique in the annals of seaside entertainment.

We are making no attempt to describe the hall, save to say that much thought and care have been lavished on its construction, and that the architect (Mr. G. H. B. Gould) and the builders (Messrs. Canler and Sons) are to be congratulated on the design, workmanship and the scheme of ventilation; and Messrs. Davison and Garrod on the artistic lighting effects. Although the new and imposing building, designated Theatre, does not add to the old seating capacity, patrons will find greater comfort by being given more "leg room ". The acoustic properties are excellent, the decorative scheme very dainty, and the setting of the fine stage an artistic achievement. In the latter connection, Mr. G. T. Mann is to be complimented.

The official opening took place on Friday evening, when a large number of residents foregathered to the " christening " of the new Theatre, and to wish the proprietors a long reign of success in their newly acquired home.

As the curtain rang up, disclosing Sir Frederick Rice, M.P., Councillor Kenneth Elliott, J.P. (Chairman of the Council) and Messrs. Graham & Bentley occupying the centre of the stage, the pianist struck the opening chords of the National Anthem in the singing of which the audience joined. Then Councillor Elliott said it was his privilege and pleasure to introduce to them Sir Frederick Rice to open that fine building Before doing so however, he took the opportunity of congratulating those pioneer entertainers—Messrs. Graham & Bentley—on moving with the times and keeping up with a progressive town, and expressed the hope that Clactonians would help the new venture in every conceivable way. (Applause).

Sir Frederick Rice said they no doubt wondered what they were going to see when the curtain rang up. (Laughter). He knew what he was going to see : a large audience to inaugurate the opening of that luxurious Theatre. When he was invited to open the Theatre by Mrs. H. Grant, who informed him that the entire proceeds would be devoted to the Clacton Hospital and the Playing Fields Association he felt it a duty, and privilege to do so, and also to pay tribute to the generous impulse of the proprietors in giving up the first fruits of their labours to the cause of charity. (Applause). He congratulated the people of Clacton and the visitors on being able to enjoy an entertainment in such luxurious surroundings, and hoped t hat the enterprise of Messrs. Graham & Bentley would meet with the generous support that it deserved, and that it would encourage them to greater effort in the future—(applause). Clacton possessed attractions unique and peculiar, and the West Cliff Gardens Theatre, he felt assured, would not be the least of those attractions. Clacton, he added in conclusion, owed much to its pioneer entertainers, who, 34 years ago, commenced their business of entertaining the visitors to the town. It was a humble start and from the chrysalis had grown the beautiful Theatre which afforded him great pleasure in declaring open. (Applause). He hoped it would be well supported, and in the way Messrs. Graham & Bentley rightly deserve for their enterprise. (Applause).

In thanking Sir Frederick and Mr. Elliott, Mr. Graham regretted the absence of Lady Rice through indisposition. He extended a cordial welcome to old and new friends to the Theatre, and assured them that as in the past so in the future they would strive to merit and retain their support and good will. This was their 35th season, and although he did not feel as agile as he did in those early days he hoped to be spared for a similar span to find visitors and residents amusement and relaxation. (Laughter and applause).

Mr. Bentley re-echoed his partner's sentiments, adding that in such palatial surroundings the company could not but rise to the occasion and excel their past efforts in the way of amusing and pleasing their patrons. (Applause).

A brief response by Sir Frederick, and the formal proceedings closed, followed, after a brief interval by the concert, which was a delightful medley of music, song, mirth, and dance, and time passed so merrily that the long programme ended all too soon. On making their initial appearances on the new stage both Mr. Graham and Mr. Bentley met with such loud and sustained applause that their make up failed to hide their blushes. Both gave of their best. Miss Emily Gardner (soprano) and Mr. Fred Gregory (baritone) sang with great acceptance. Mr. Fred Gibson and Miss Nance Haines provided humour rich and rare. Miss Cythna Dell & Miss Geraldine Schuster delighted the audience with their dances. The sketches, in which all the company shared, were very amusing. Miss Kathleen O'Hagan was the accomplished pianist.

Throughout the week the programmes have been varied, and the audiences have come away delighted with the "bill of fare."

Photo by]   [N. K. Harrison

The Interior of the new West Cliff Gardens Theatre.

The West Cliff Theatre is built

The next big step forward came in 1928 when Messrs Graham and Bentley submitted plans to the Clacton Urban District Council for a new "Concert Pavilion" designed by Mr G.W. Gould, architect, of Station Road, Clacton. Approval was readily given and the building work was carried out by local builders Canler and Sons.

The new theatre was officially opened on 25th May 1928 by Sir Frederick Rice M.P. In replying to Sir Frederick's speech, Will Bentley commented that "in such palatial surroundings the company could not but rise to the occasion and excel their past efforts in the way of amusing and pleasing their patrons." Incidentally, it is interesting to note in passing that 1928 was also the year the Ocean Theatre on the Pier was opened, so the West Cliff was faced with some stiff opposition right from the start.

Since its opening there have been a number of changes made to the theatre, but it is basically still the same building as the one in use today. In recognition of this fact and in honour of its founders, the letters "G" and "B" (for Graham and Bentley) can still be seen picked out above the proscenium arch.

For the opening show at the new theatre the Company was still billed as the London Concert Company and, as well as the two producers, included the husband and wife team of Fred Gibson and Nance Haines, Kathleen O'Hagan, Emily Gardner, Geraldine Schoster, Cynthia Dell and Fred Gregory.

The Summer Seasons continued in their new purpose-built theatre with performers such as Fred Good, Winfred Scott, Norman Long, Murray Ashford and, in 1933, the last year under the direction of Graham and Bentley, Ernie Leno, son of the immortal Dan Leno, appearing in shows like Sunshine and

The West Cliff Theatre nearing completion in 1928

Laughter, Entertainers and Crazy People. Special one-off concerts were also held with big name stars appearing including, in 1929, the Western Brothers and in 1932, Leslie Sarony.

As many local residents as holidaymakers used to watch the shows. And indeed, the locals had their favourite seats and could become very irate if they found they had been sold to a holidaymaker!

From Tuesday March 18th to Saturday March 22nd, as a curtain raiser to the 1930 summer season, the West Cliff Gardens Theatre put on the first ever performance by the Clacton Amateur Operatic Society. Six performances of The Pirates of Penzance were staged (including a matinee on Saturday). This starred Herbert Bischoff as Major General Stanley, Henry Learoyd (the headmaster of St Osyth Road Primary School) as the Pirate King, Leonard Pease as Frederic, Henry C. Cole as the Sergeant of Police and Edie Bush as Mabel.

This was the first time that the West Cliff had been used out of season and consequently there was no proper heating laid on. The audience sat through the performances with blankets covering their laps!

Messrs Graham and Bentley were Vice-Presidents of the Operatic Society along with many other prominent Clactonians of the time, including the M.P. and Minister for Transport, Mr John Pybus, Mr Douglas Lewellen, Mr Robert Coan and many others.

WEST CLIFF THEATRE

West Cliff Gardens Theatre (Clacton) Ltd.
Licensee: WILL HAMMER.   Manager: BERT GRAHAM.
Est. 1894.   'Phone 107.

WILL HAMMER
presents

THE 1934 CLACTON ENTERTAINERS

Jack Rickards

Fred Wildon

GAZETTE, SATURDAY, JUNE 30, 1928.

NS : Scenes in Town

THE WESTCLIFF GARDENS THEATRE COMPANY.

Left to right: Fred Gibson, Nance Haines, Kathleen O'Hagan, Will Bentley, Emily Gardner, Bert Graham, Cythna Dell, Geraldine Schuster and Frederic Gregory.   (Photo by Leith, Jetty Studio.

BEAUTY AND GRACE ON CLACTON BEACH.

Stanley Holloway

CLACTON AMATEUR OPERATIC SOCIETY

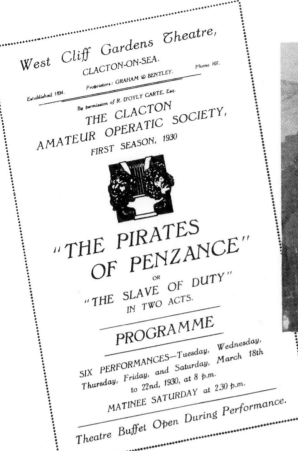

Although the photo is *The Pirates of Penzance,* this is the 1936 production. CAOS's 12th show.

" We began the Clacton Amateur Operatic Society in 1930. Auditions were held in St Osyth Road School. The headmaster, Harry Learoyd, was a founder member. He had a very powerful voice and played the Pirate King in our first production, The Pirates of Penzance.

The West Cliff Theatre at that time was fairly new and rather primitive. As there were normally no shows other than the Summer Season there was no heating laid on. So when we put on our first performance, in March 1930, before the season opened, the theatre was very cold. The audience sat through the show with blankets on their laps.

The dressing rooms were also a bit sparse and in fact the men's dressing room was in the loft and they had to get up and down by means of a ladder.

However, we stayed on at the West Cliff and particularly after Will Hammer took over in 1934 we had a very good relationship with the theatre. Will Hammer was a good friend to the CAOS and later to the CADS when that was formed after the war."

Phyl Gascoigne

Founder member and President of
The Clacton Amateur Dramatic Society

Under the Hammer!

Throughout the 1920s and early 30s, Will Bentley was trying to cope with running two successful businesses. As well as the West Cliff Theatre, he also ran a thriving Oyster Restaurant in Piccadilly in the heart of London. Every day he caught the early morning commuter train up to town, returning on the evening train just in time to change and go on at the West Cliff. By the time 1934 came around he had decided to concentrate on his oyster business.

To begin the 1934 season Graham and Bentley put on a show called Will Hammer's Entertainers. Shortly afterwards, in April 1934, in line with Will Bentley's wishes, the pair of them put the West Cliff up for sale by auction at Ernest Johnson's and the theatre was sold to the same Will Hammer whose show they had begun the season by producing. Will Hammer, a theatrical agent, whose real name was William Hinds, already owned several theatres around the coast, including one at Felixstowe, as well as a large number of jewellery stores, hairdressing salons and bicycle shops.

Will Bentley now retired from the theatre to spend more time with his oyster business, while Bert Graham stayed on as manager of the theatre. This was to last for just one season as in November 1934 he too decided to call it a day. On his retirement he was presented with a hammered pewter cigarette box by the girl attendants. Bert Graham remained in Clacton for many years to run his high-class confectionery shop firstly in West Avenue and then in Jackson Road.

It was the Jackson Road shop that was to be the later setting for a nostalgic and poignant moment in 1959 when Stanley Holloway, by then an internationally known star, in town for the funeral of Ethel Bentley, (Will's widow), visited his old boss and mentor, the 86 year old Bert Graham, last surviving member of the Graham, Russell and Bentley partnership.

"My first recollection of the West Cliff Theatre was in the summer of 1923 when, as a boy of 10 years of age, I was taken by my mother and father to see the show put on by Graham and Bentley.

Little did I know that 17 years later I was to marry Phyllis who was the daughter of Lilian Graham (Bert Graham's sister) who had appeared in the original shows!"

John H. Groves

"I was in Clacton in the Summer of 1934 with my future husband, John H. Groves, when we visited my uncle, Bert Graham, at the West Cliff Theatre one afternoon. As we were having tea in the foyer my uncle was called away. On his return he told us that somebody had approached him with a view to buying the theatre, which offer took him completely by surprise.

We found out later that he sold the theatre to Will Hammer, but continued as theatre manager for a while before retiring and opening a high class confectioners locally.

My mother was Lilian Graham (Bert's sister), who was a singer and member of the original London Concert Company."

Phyllis Groves
Bert Graham's niece

Will Hammer
(1887 – 1957)

Will Hammer, whose real name was William Hinds, had many interests besides the West Cliff Theatre. As well as being a theatrical agent employing a string of Music Hall artistes, he owned a chain of jewellery shops, (some with hairdressing salons above) and, as a keen amateur cyclist himself, a number of bicycle shops. He adopted the name Hammer as a contraction of Hammersmith, where he lived and where he owned one of his jewellery shops.

He owned or rented several seaside theatres, which he either ran on his own or in conjunction with the band leader, Jack Payne. He also liked to appear in as many of his own shows as he could as a comedian.

A very shy and reserved man off stage, he nevertheless nursed a great ambition to become famous. This ambition was eventually gratified when, following a meeting with a man called Enrique Carreras, a cinema owner, the two of them founded a film distribution company called Exclusive Films Ltd. in the early 1930s.

In the same year that he bought the West Cliff, Will Hammer also founded another film company called Hammer Productions Ltd. with himself as Chairman. The Company produced five films, including the Mystery of the Marie Celeste and The Song of Freedom, in which Hammer took a small part.

Hammer Productions Ltd went out of business shortly before the war, but in 1947, his other company, Exclusive Films re-issued all five films. This encouraged Hammer to reform his production company and so, in 1949, Hammer Film Productions Ltd. was founded with Will Hammer, Enrique Carreras and their two sons, Anthony Hinds and James Carreras as directors.

Although their early films were mainly routine adventure yarns, e.g., Dick Barton, Special Agent and The Man in Black, it was with the subsequent making of The Curse of Frankenstein in 1956 and Dracula in 1957, that Hammer's name became synonymous with horror all over the world.

Although Hammer himself died in 1957, following a cycling accident, his name lives on to this day in the company he gave his name to. The Hammer House of Horror may be a far cry from the family atmosphere of the West Cliff Theatre, Clacton, but it has undoubtedly achieved Hammer's ambition of becoming a household name!

Will Hammer's first innovation at the West Cliff was to keep the theatre open all the year round with a mixture of variety, concert parties, pantomime and repertory companies. His first show took place at Whitsun, 1934, and starred the Roosters, an all-male concert party, who, according to the East Essex Gazette, were "World famous, needing no introduction to Clacton audiences as they had already been heard on radio and gramophone records". Prices for the show were 2/6d, 1/10d and 1/3d, with a "limited number" at 7d. Children half-price.

However, it was still the Summer Season which provided the theatre-s bread and butter with shows such as West End Vanities, Revelry at The West Cliff and Vaudeville at The West Cliff and performers that included Jack

Rowlands, Gordon Marsh, Tubby Harold and Kathleen Price.

For one-off shows, he was able to attract a number of the top stars of the thirties to the West Cliff, including Bennett & Williams, Albert Whelan, Harry Tate and Robb Wilton. But it was while the 1939 summer season – Swingtime at The West Cliff – was in full swing that proceedings came to an abrupt end when, on 2nd September, all theatres closed on the outbreak of the second world war.

Fortunately however the theatre was able to re-open on 2nd October for a non-stop variety show starring Pam and Nibs, Clement Minus, Videau & King and the Milson Sisters with shows taking place once a week for a while. During the war, shows continued at the theatre on a one night stand basis, mostly E.N.S.A. shows for the forces, as for most of the war Clacton was a front line town with thousands of troops stationed in and around the town.

Will Hammer re-opened the Summer Season at the West Cliff in 1946 with a show called Victory Vanities in which he himself starred with comedienne Ivy Esta. 1947 saw Nosmo King starring in a show called For the Fun of It with a young up-and-coming comedian having his first ever summer season, one Frankie Howerd.

Harry Tate in his famous sketch, Motoring, appeared at the West Cliff Theatre in 1938

Firemen on the roof after putting out the blaze at the Theatre on 12th July, 1950

CLACTON AMATEUR DRAMATIC SOCIETY

The CADS first production
Berkeley Square in 1947

Also in 1947 the Clacton Amateur Dramatic Society (CADS) made their debut at The West Cliff. After some earlier preliminary discussions, the CADS took definite shop when Phyl and John Gascoigne, Cyril Harman and Jo St Clair got together in the latter's shop, Peggoty's, in Electric Parade (Pier Avenue) to discuss a formal constitution. Their first performance, Berkeley Square, was put on in February 1947 during one of the worst wintry spells on record. Those present on the occasion of the first night can still remember the snow blowing into the theatre through the vents in the roof!

1950 saw drama of another kind at the West Cliff when a fire damaged much of the area backstage. It started when two mattresses caught fire in a loft used as a temporary store and spread quickly destroying the grid, battens, ropes and pulleys, scenery, tabs and curtains. One of the Tom Katz Saxophone Six also lost his brand new saxophone for which he had just paid £85.

The fire began at approximately 5:45 p.m. on Wednesday 12th July, but following a lot of hard work by the cast and local workmen, the show was ready to re-open for the Saturday performance. Will Hammer himself came down for the performance and afterwards took the stage to thank the whole town for its help during and after the fire, especially the neighbours who had brought tea, the hoteliers who had sent up sandwiches, Billy Nelson ('The 60" Comedian') who had found the fire and the girls of the Company who had dived into the smoke filled dressing rooms to save their frocks and properties.

Hammer continued to produce his annual summer revue until his death following a cycling accident in 1957. Some of the starts to appear during this period were Alec Pleon, Bunny Baron, Jack Francis and Joe Black in shows like Sunshine and Smiles (produced jointly with band leader Jack Payne), Joy Bells, Come to the Show and Fine and Dandy.

The Theatre in
Coronation Year, 1953

The theatre is saved

By the time of Hammer's death, the theatre, now nearly 30 years old, was falling into a state of disrepair and was beginning to look rather the worse for wear. With audiences generally beginning to drop off, due in some measure to the influence of television, it began to look doubtful if a buyer with the necessary capital to invest would be found to buy the theatre. At one time it looked possible that The West Cliff would be lost altogether as the North East Metropolitan Regional Hospital Board expressed an interest in the site for use as an extension to Clacton Hospital.

No plans were made by the Hammer Organisation for a 1958 season, but in July of that Year, the Band Pavilion ran into financial trouble and had to be bailed out by Clacton Council, who took over the running of the show and decided to replace Raymond Kerry's revue with the popular Ronnie Mills. Raymond Kerry then leased the West Cliff and late in July transferred his show, The Rayker Revue, for what was left of the Summer Season.

At the end of the 1958 season discussions took place over the future of The West Cliff. Councillor Jo St. Clair, a leading light in the Clacton Amateur Operatic Society as well as the Clacton Amateur Dramatic Society, together with a number of prominent councillors, led a campaign to get Clacton Urban District Council itself to make an offer for the Theatre. There was a great deal of opposition from other councillors who proposed that the Theatre should be demolished and a block of flats built in its place. Following an exciting debate in full Council, the move to purchase the Theatre was carried by the narrowest of margins.

This decision caused uproar in the town. Objections were raised by the East Ward Ratepayers Association as well as by the owners of Clacton Pier and the Savoy Theatre. The former on the grounds that it was a waste of ratepayers money, the latter on the grounds that it would affect their business. In support of the Council, however, the Secretary of the Clacton Hotel, Guest House and Restaurant Association stated that the members of his general committee were unanimously in support of the proposal.

The matter was finally decided at a public inquiry chaired by Mr W.H. Norris from the Ministry of Housing and Local Government held in Clacton Town Hall on 19th February 1959, where the council's decision was upheld. The cost of the venture was £7000 for the Theatre plus £750 for fixtures and fittings. For the first and only time in its history, the Theatre remained dark for a whole year as the formal legalities were gone through, but eventually on 24th August 1959, West Cliff Gardens Theatre (Clacton) Ltd was signed over to Clacton Urban District Council.

With the Council now in charge, a decision was made to stop putting on the traditional Summer Variety show as there were already a number of other shows of this type in Clacton. For example, the Savoy Theatre, the Ocean Theatre, the Band Pavilion and the Ramblas open air concert party on the Pier were all actively engaged in presenting Summer Variety shows. Therefore in an attempt to appeal to a different kind of audience and to increase the potential of Clacton as a holiday resort, it was decided to change direction and put on a repertory season in 1960.

This proved to be so successful that the repertory seasons were continued for several years with The Penguin Players starring Rex Deering, who had run the Rambla Concert Party on the Pier before the war, having two seasons and the Galleon Theatre Company having three seasons at the West Cliff with a change of play each week. In 1966, a Brian Rix presentation took place when One for the Pot alternated with Wanted – One Body for the summer season. These plays starred Jerry Desmonde, George Moon and Bill Treacher (Arthur Fowler in television's Eastenders).

"I can very well remember when Clacton Council took the Theatre over there was a whole lot of poor seating, so we ripped it all out and took up the concrete. We had to do that because it was so brittle. I can remember standing on the virgin soil below the surface of the present floor before they re-concreted it in order to be able to bolt in the lovely new seating we still have today.

Since then there have been various extensions. Perhaps one of the main extensions has been the stage. We had to bring it right over the orchestra pit because some of the dance routines, the girls with all their feathers and so on, are so spectacular that you need that extra area, rather like a London theatre or a big provincial theatre.

Of course, I was very involved in advertising and organising publicity for Clacton as a holiday resort in those days and naturally we used the West Cliff as one of the town's major attractions. For example the year Tommy Trinder was here enabled us to get on the radio, on television and get talked about everywhere. That was the year (1972) that we advertised on the buses for the first time.

Although Tommy's show didn't bring in the crowds, he more than made up for it by what he did for the town. He went round opening fetes, bazaars, sporting events and so on. In fact he said himself that he opened everything in Clacton except a hole in the road! And, not only that, but he did it all for nothing and so willingly. He even drove everywhere himself because he said he didn't want to be any bother to us. So, although directly he didn't draw the crowds, indirectly he gained us enormous publicity and goodwill.

I was also involved with the decision in 1973 to bring Francis Golightly in to produce the summer shows. This was probably one of the best decisions of my career with the Council. Francis is a great improviser with great ingenuity, drive and enthusiasm and his success at The West Cliff has been well-deserved."

Harry Thompson

Former Clacton Council and Tendring Council
Publicity and Entertainments Manager

With the closure of the Savoy Theatre and the Ramblas show and with the Band Pavilion no longer producing summer shows, the way was clear for the West Cliff to once again return to Variety in 1967 with Bunny Baron being asked to produce the summer season. This he did with a show entitled Starnite Spectacular. starring Don MacLean, a young entertainer he had spotted the previous season at Felixstowe.

Throughout this period the Council put a lot of effort into advertising and publicity in an attempt to bring audiences into the West Cliff but audiences fluctuated and in 1972 Baron decided to bring in a top name star in an attempt to win back the crowds. But even Tommy Trinder failed to draw the crowds and whole question of the future of the West Cliff was once again in the balance, with calls being made in the local press for the theatre to be demolished and the money saved spent on a marina or dry ski slope.

"1967 was momentous for me. It was my first season as principal comic. Bunny Baron had seen me appearing in a small show at Felixstowe the previous summer and he gave me a chance. He paid me £45 per week. (Don't tell Francis, he'll expect me to work for the same money!) It was also the first year Toni and I were married. We'd got wed the previous February, so, all in all, a very happy year.

We thought up a few stunts to interest the local paper and hopefully get publicity for the show. One of those was breakfast on the beach, in fact in the sea. I enclose a snapshot. The chap at the front with moustache is Harry Dickman who has gone on to appear in numerous musicals, including 42nd Street and Pirates of Penzance in the West End and also the RSC production of Pyjama Game. The blonde was our head girl, Janice Peeling, who became well known as a choreographer under the name of Jan Linton.

1984 was a super season. Francis puts on such a good show. During that season I learned to fly at Clacton Airfield and I'll be bringing my aeroplane over with me this summer.

In 1967 the best seats cost 6/6d (32.5p). In 1984, £2.95p.In 1994 they were £7.50 and this year (2008) they'll be £12.50.

God Bless"

Don Maclean

The latest phase

However, the Council decided to keep faith with the idea of live theatrical entertainment and following discussions between Harry Thompson, on behalf of Clacton Council and Francis Golightly, who offered to stage a summer show without star names but offering "colour, music and spectacle," The West Cliff continued in 1973 under a new director.

Francis Golightly has continued to run the summer season ever since at the West Cliff with shows such as Showtime, Holiday Startime and Cascade Revue.

Although, at one time, in 1976, an offer was received from John Redgrave to put on the summer shows in Clacton as he was doing at the time in Eastbourne with a great deal of success, the Council decided to stick with Francis Golightly and the good relationship built up between Harry Thompson and Francis Golightly has paid excellent dividends for the theatre as right from the start Tendring District Council (the successors to Clacton Council) have put a lot of effort - not to mention money - into supporting the shows, while for his part Francis Golightly himself has put such effort into producing just the right sort of show to appeal to both holidaymakers and residents alike that he has often been credited with "having done more to secure the future of the West Cliff Theatre than anyone else."

Some of the names to have appeared in Francis Golightly's time include not only established stars such as Kenny Cantor, Billy Dainty, Rosemary Squires, Don Maclean, Norman Collier and Peter Goodwright, but Francis has also been responsible for discovering some of Britain's brightest young entertainers and giving them their first taste of success at the West Cliff. Names in this category include Gary Wilmot, Alex Bourne and Ruthie Henshall.

"Before the advent of holidays abroad most families enjoyed a week or two at one of the many seaside resorts around the coast of Britain.
An essential part of the holiday was the entertainment provided in venues such as the West Cliff in Clacton. Famous shows like Twinkle, The Fol de Rols and Clacton's Ocean Revue returned to the resorts year after year.
We are told that in the summer of 1948, around eight o'clock in the evening 200 pianos would be crashing out the opening choruses of these special summer shows throughout the length and breadth of the British Isles. Summer entertainment was unique and entirely different from the music hall and variety shows to be found in the theatres. Floral Halls, Winter Gardens, Pier Pavilions all had their own brand of humour.

It was noticeable in editions of This Is Your Life on t.v how time and time again those who were appearing related how they first appeared in concert parties as a start of their careers. They all agreed that there was no finer training ground for their profession than periods spent at the seaside. Fortunately we still have a few, a very few, venues offering first class entertainment for holidaymakers and the management of the West Cliff Theatre are to be congratulated on still keeping the flag flying for this kind of enjoyable entertainment. Long may they continue to flourish."

Max Tyler

(Max Tyler is the British Music Hall Society's official historian)

"When I first came along in '73 it was my first professional summer season. Prior to that I'd been producing amateur shows in Braintree and I cam along and found this rather damp theatre that had an awful smell to it. There was no heating and so on and so forth.

It was always the poor relation to the Ocean Theatre because the theatre was – and still is – in a residential part of the town away from the mainstream of holidaymakers.

I came with a show costing £828 a week for the whole package. What I felt was lacking previously was the glamour, the feathers, the tinsel and that's what I put into the theatre. We never went in for star names and, in fact, we filled the place. We broke every record in the first year, 1973. The business which had traditionally packed the Ocean Theatre, much to everybody's surprise, came to the West Cliff. Phrases like "The West Cliff reborn" were frequently used.

Against all the odds this was the start of a new lease of life for this lovely theatre. The David and Goliath situation had been reversed and the West Cliff Theatre became the success story that has continued right through to the present day.

The formation of the West Cliff Trust, who take care of the theatre during the autumn, winter and spring, and its combination with the well established summer season is part of the success story. But we must never lost sight of the fact that without the financial support and certainly the good will of Tendring District Council the whole business just wouldn't be viable."

Francis Golightly

"We first started our double act in 1950 when a young people's group, of which we were members, formed a concert party and the organisers decided they needed some comedy to add variety to the singing and dancing. First using material we had garnered from our visits to the various Sunday shows being produced in Clacton at that time, we soon adopted our own style and were very popular at the holiday camps and hotels in the area.

But our happiest times on the stage have been since 1995, as it was in that year that we began providing Sunday afternoon variety shows at the West Cliff to raise money for the theatre (around £30,000 to date) and to give newcomers and young performers an opportunity to showcase their talents to a larger audience. We are glad to say these shows continue to this day and regularly sell-out the theatre.

God bless the dear old West Cliff!"

Reg and Bob Young

"Why has the West Cliff survived when so many other seaside theatres have bitten the dust? Well, success in show business has always been down to individuals. Those out of the ordinary, slightly mad people who implicitly trust their own judgement and somehow seem to know, even anticipate, just what the public want. The West Cliff has had more than its share of special people from Bert Graham and Will Bentley through Will Hammer to the flamboyant showman, Francis Golightly and now John Warwick.

It had, and still has, an ever growing group of friends. The Friends of the West Cliff Theatre. In the theatre's darkest days these were the folk who did the maintenance, raised funds, became ushers, talked about and encouraged audiences to come to their beloved pavilion. More to the point they continue to do it. With friends like these and the Trust a successful future seems assured.

The little theatre has always inspired great affection from all who sit in its auditorium and from those who entertain from its stage. I had the great joy of being part of the Water Rats show organised by Don Smoothey and Len Lowe which finally enabled the roof to be made safe in 1990. It was a very proud moment when the Rats agreed, backstage, to hand over their share of the profits to the Roofing Fund.

A happy birthday West Cliff – we all love you."

Roy Hudd

Roy Hudd

John Warwick

The Theatre in April 1990, before retiling the roof. *Photo: Tony Ellis*

Although the Summer Show was flourishing there was little other activity at the theatre during the rest of the year and what there was were mainly amateur productions from CADS and CAOS, and by the early 80s there were murmurings in the press and elsewhere that the Council were spending too much ratepayers' money on keeping open a theatre that was essentially only used for eight weeks of the year and there was a very real possibility that Tendring District Council (TDC), the successor to Clacton Urban District Council, might pull the plug on its funding thereby effectively closing the theatre. In view of this threat, two prominent members of CAOS, Mike Freeman and Peter Anselmi, decided to form a group to rally public opinion and to put pressure on the council to continue to support the West Cliff.

And so the Tendring Theatre Association (TTA) was formed from local theatre users and business people and included, as well as Mike and Peter, Keith Pollard, Des Pye, Alan King, George Osborne, Francis Golightly and Harry Thompson and organisations such as CADS, CAOS, Clacton Theatregoers Association, Choral Society and Frinton Summer Theatre.

With the full support of the community, the TTA then approached Tendring District Council with plans for making use of the theatre all year round and for the Association itself to become more involved with the day-to-day running of the theatre. Following a detailed submission of their plans to the Council, it was agreed by TDC that the Association be asked to form a Trust jointly with the Council (six members from the TTA and three from the Council) to take over the running of the Theatre outside the Summer Season as "This is likely to be the best chance available for this District to establish a centre for the Arts which would seem a highly desirable addition to our way of life." [TDC report, 10 January 1985]

To help turn the theatre in to an all year round venue, the Council gave a grant of £20,000 to insulate the building and to install a heating system. Part of the grant was also to go to improving the bar area to enable it to provide food and snacks and the rest was to upgrade the foyer area for art and photographic exhibitions, turning it from just a theatre to a theatre and arts centre.

It was hoped that ultimately a complete new

annexe would be built providing a meeting and rehearsal room, increased bar space and additional toilets and showers so that a comprehensive centre for all kinds of artistic, theatrical and commercial activities would be provided.

Because there were just nine Trust members, all of whom had other full-time jobs, to do everything that needed to be done, it was felt that a new organisation was needed to help raise money, publicise the theatre and carry out the front of house and back-stage jobs and so the Friends of the West Cliff Theatre was formed in 1987.

With the Trust and Friends now dedicated to making a success of the theatre, the number of shows put on at the theatre expanded as once again it became a full-time all-year round venue with star names such as the late Roy Castle, Bobby Davro, Roy Hudd and Bucks Fizz; theatre companies such as the Compass Theatre Company and Hull Truck Theatre Company; a variety of events, including ballet, music hall, jazz, opera and rock 'n' roll and many other different forms of entertainment including puppet shows, pantomimes and even illustrated talks on aspects of Clacton's history while CADS and CAOS also continued to put on their shows at the theatre.

Indeed, so much activity was now taking place the time had come to employ a professional full-time administrator. With Eastern Arts agreeing to pay half the salary, Adrian Towler was appointed to the post in 1989, initially on a three year contract, which was later extended.

In 1990 it became apparent that the roof of the theatre was in urgent need of repair and an appeal was launched to raise £25,000. After a tremendous amount of work by the Friends and members of the Trust and with the support of a number of top entertainers such as George Melly, Gorden Kaye, Roy Hudd and The Grand Order of Water Rats the money was found and the roof repaired.

After nearly ten years of showing that it could run the West Cliff as a successful all year round theatre and arts centre, the Trust contacted the Council with a view to buying the freehold of the theatre outright. Following detailed negotiations Tendring District Council offered to sell the theatre to the Trust, on condition that they (the Council) continued to run the Summer Season. This was agreed and in 1995, the West Cliff (Tendring) Trust became the new freeholders.

Francis Golightly continued to produce the Summer Season on behalf of Tendring District Council until 2001, when he produced his last Cascade Revue. The agreement that the Council itself should be responsible for the summer show ended with Francis Golightly's last season and from 2002 onwards the Trustees became responsible for putting on the show and finding a producer, although it was still a condition of TDC's grant that a summer show be staged with a "star name".

In 2002, Open Wide Productions, the company responsible for the successful Cromer Pier Summer Shows, took over the running of the summer season, while in 2004 there was a departure from the normal format when the Derek Grant Organisation produced a season that saw a different star for each day of the week, so that you could see Joan Regan on Wednesdays throughout the summer, Vince Hill on Thursdays, Maggie Moone on Fridays and Stan Stennett and Peter Hudson on Saturdays. However, the experiment was not a success and since 2005, the summer season has reverted to the normal formula, produced by John Warwick with names such as Jimmy Cricket and Bernie Clifton.

As the theatre now celebrates 80 years of the present building it is with some pride that the Trust and Friends can point to the continuing success of the Summer Show. At one time, every seaside resort in the country had at least one Summer Show – Clacton itself could boast at least three or four between the 1930s and 60s – now the West Cliff is one of only a handful of theatres around the country, maybe six or seven, still putting on this traditional form of British entertainment, while during the rest of the year, the number and variety of shows continues to grow.

As well as being a Theatre and Arts Centre, the West Cliff has, in recent years, placed itself at the heart of the Tendring Community by playing host to a number of organisations who use its facilities on a regular basis, such as the Lions, Clacton Rotary Club, the 41 Club, Age Concern and the Cavaliers for example as well as hosting a number of major events, including a Tendring History Fair, which involved local societies from the whole of Tendring, the Essex Archaeological and Historical Congress AGM, a Crime Prevention Evening, a Salvation Army Youth Assembly and as the focal point for the public consultation over the Clacton town centre regeneration scheme. In particular the theatre is proud of its support for local schools in holding joint projects with them as well as providing them facilities for their drama and media students to learn both front and back stage skills, a venue for prize giving ceremonies and a place for them to hold examinations.

In all the West Cliff Theatre is in use for something like 300 days a year, something that the founders Bert Graham, Bernard Russell and Will Bentley would have considered a flight of fancy. But, no doubt, if the three men were able to come back today, they would be very proud to see what has become of their creation and to see the massive part it now plays in the lives of all who live in Clacton and the wider Tendring area.

The West Cliff Stage Foundation

The group was formed in 2000 with their first appearance in public being at the Tendring Show that year.

Since that time they have continued to put on at least one show every year at the West Cliff. See below for the complete list. As well as these productions the group has appeared at the Tendring Show, the Air Show, the Princes Theatre and have performed in other shows at the West Cliff, for example, the Young Brothers' show.

The members of the Stage Foundation range in age from 11 – 18 years and, as well as learning the normal front of stage skills such as acting, singing and dancing there are also workshops covering specialist skills including clog dancing, ballet and magic. Backstage skills are also taught, including painting and design and puppet making.

The number of students now attending sessions is just over 35 with a waiting list of those wishing to get in. When a production is in rehearsal they meet twice weekly and more frequently as the production date looms.

The director of the foundation is Penelope Game, one of the Theatre's Trustees. She is supported by Chris Bareham.

Productions

2001: Centenary (A young person's view of the past 100 years)

2001: Fifties Fever (A holiday camp romp)

2002: Celebration (Like the first two productions, written by a staff member)

2002: The Frankenstein Monster Show (The group's first professionally written piece)

2003: Oliver

2003: In the Spotlight (A variety show with original ideas from the students)

2004: Peter Pan

2005: Half a Sixpence

2006: The Wizard of Oz

2007: Guys and Dolls

2008: Summer Holiday

The West Cliff Stage Foundation on a photo shoot with a big red London bus for their 2008 production of Summer Holiday.

George Melly, on behalf of the Theatre, accepts a generous donation of £6,000 from Tendring District Council for the Roof Appeal. December 1990.

Mike Freeman lays the last tile on the roof, April 1991. Photo: Tony Ellis

The Friends of the West Cliff Theatre

"The West Cliff (Tendring) Trust Ltd was formed in 1985 and comprised ten members, of whom two were Tendring District Councillors and one a Tendring District Council chief officer. The rest of the Trust was made up of representatives of the local Operatic and Dramatic societies together with Francis Golightly.

The first major problem which faced the Trust was to make the Theatre user-friendly both summer and winter. Top priority was therefore given to the installation of a heating system. By 1987 it was obvious that Many more improvements were essential to make the theatre habitable and an active fund raising body was needed and thus the Friends of the West Cliff was born in July of that year. The first committee was formed and a sum of £50 was borrowed from the Trust to cover initial administrative costs. Never has there been a better investment – within weeks the Friends had raised their first £1000, at a fete. They repaid the £50 and have never looked back.

During the last twenty one years many thousands of pounds has been raised by the Friends and almost all the changes and improvements at the Theatre bear witness as to how the money has been spent, the most recent being the vast improvement to the foyer, Friends' shop and the bar area; also the security lighting outside the building. Looking to the future many more exciting projects are currently in the pipeline to be funded by money raised by the Friends.

As well as being superb fund raisers, the Friends provide an army of volunteers who act as Front of House staff, showing people to their seats, sell ice-cream and sweets, run the gift shop and ensure the safety of the Theatre. They also organise a coffee morning every Saturday at which funds are raised by selling coffee as well as second-hand books where friends can get together for a pleasant social morning in a congenial atmosphere. The more technically minded help with the sound and lighting while still others turn their hand to painting and decorating. Some indeed do several of these jobs.

Finally, we have a band of postmen who deliver newsletters and publicity around the area, thus saving a great deal of money. All in all a most dedicated group of Friends whom I am delighted to call my friends."

Janet Price

Founder secretary of the
Friends of the West Cliff Theatre

The Young brothers with Jimmy Cricket

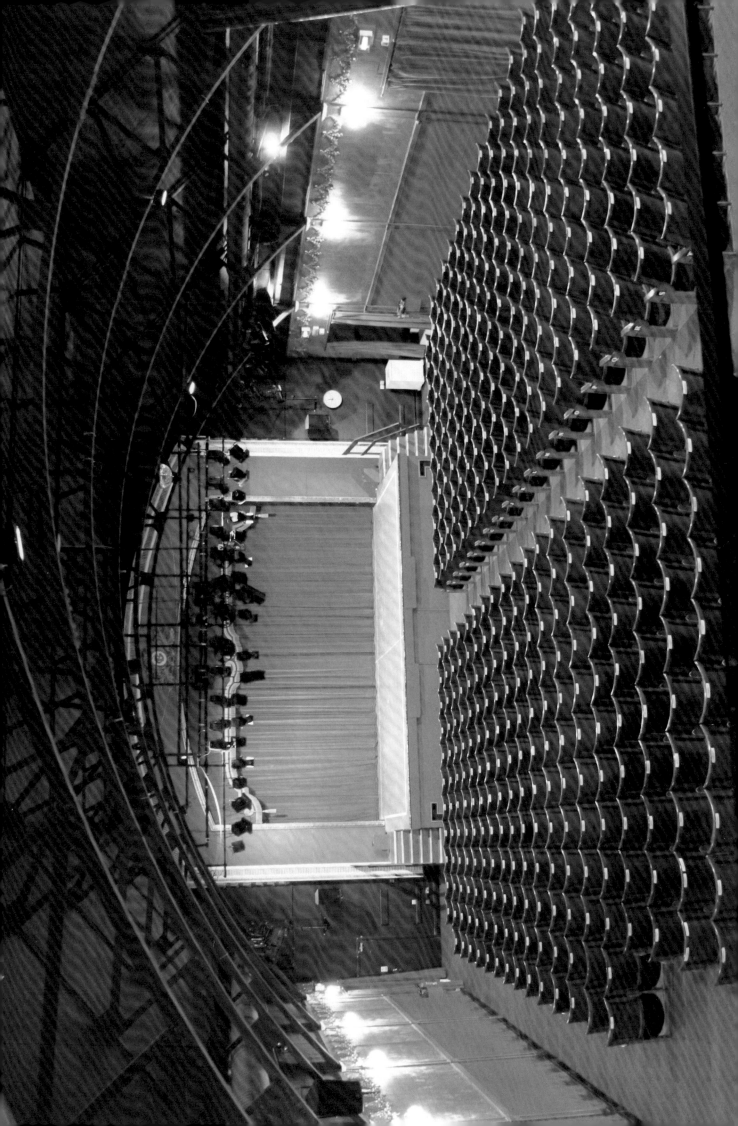

The West Cliff (Tendring) Trust Ltd.

"I am extremely please to be involved in this second edition of the West Cliff Story as it marks yet another chapter in the Theatre's history charting a further 15 years of Trust ownership.

When we started this venture in 1985, we only dreamed of a Theatre that would open throughout the year and provide a varied and viable programme of entertainment. We truly had no clear idea of how this could be achieved, only the belief that it would be worthwhile.

And worthwhile it has proved to be, with more people being entertained in our Theatre than ever before and being open for over 320 days a year compared to the 90 or so when we started.. That success is largely due to the help, support and, sometimes literally, the blood, sweat and tears of my fellow Trustees and the army of Friends and volunteers who organise and staff the West Cliff and we are fortunate to have Norman Jacobs as a Trustee and an experienced author and historian to chart our progress.

I should at this point record our thanks to Tendring District Council who had the vision to support us in the early days and continue that support today. I only hope we can count on a modest financial contribution for the future, as this venue has become vital to the lives of so many of Tendring's young and old population.

It is fitting that in the year we celebrated 100 years of live entertainment we looked forward to the beginning of the next important phase in the Theatre's life, when the Trust purchased the freehold of the West Cliff from Tendring District Council. This meant that the Theatre was returned once more into private ownership where it thrived in its early days. It also means that the wider interests of our Community have become involved and influenced by our development. We proudly claim that the West Cliff is "at the heart of the Tendring Community" and it certainly is with dozens of groups using the Theatre for meetings, meals, gallery displays and performances every month.

A particularly gratifying change has been the involvement of young people. This

District council Chairman Percy Rayner hands over the keys of the West Cliff Theatre to the chairman of the new theatre trust, Michael Freeman.

ranges from free seats for our Summer and Winter Shows to the establishment of the West Cliff Theatre Stage Foundation. Here, young people from a variety of backgrounds are taught theatre skills and rehearse for an annual show. The standards are high and none are turned away. A spin off from the Foundation is the increasing use of youngsters on the technical side of performances. Technicians are always in demand and a recently introduced "buddy" training system is taking them from novices to fully trained operators.

Our connections with local schools continue to strengthen with joint projects, competitions and examinations being held alongside prize givings. We offer a mature and professional venue for the many local students who study the performing arts and media.

The tradition of live theatre on Clacton 's west cliff started all those years ago and we aim to see that it continues for at least another 100 years in spite of Television, DVD's, The Internet and Mobile Communications. We see these technologies as tools not our downfall and will embrace change because we believe there is no substitute for a live performance.

Running a small theatre was not easy 100 years ago and nothing has changed. But the sheer thrill and satisfaction gained when the HOUSE FULL board goes out made it all worthwhile then and still does today.

All of us connected with the West Cliff are dedicated to ensuring that it is secure for the next 100 years and continues to provide the Tendring community with a programme of high quality and varied entertainment and arts events and a place to meet, to chat and to enjoy the arts.

I would love to be there!"

Mike Freeman

Chairman,
West Cliff (Tendring) Trust, 1994

The West Cliff (Tendring) Trust buy the freehold of the Theatre from Tendring District Council

West Cliff Summer Shows 1928 – 2008

Year	Name	Stars	Producer
1928	New and Up-to-Date	Fred Gibson, Nance Haines, Bert Graham, Will Bentley	Bert Graham & Will Bentley
1929	Lido Follies	Len Clifford, Connie Rhude, Booth Hitchen	Bert Graham & Will Bentley by arrangement with Archie Pitt
1930	Sunshine & Laughter	Bert Graham & Will Bentley	Graham & Bentley
1931	Murray Ashford's Entertainers	Fred Good, Winifred Scott	Murray Ashford
1932	Murray Ashford's Entertainers	Norman Long	Murray Ashford
1933	Crazy People	Ernie Leno, Murray Ashford	John Berryman and Adele Wesseley
1934	Clacton Entertainers of 1934	Jack Richards	Will Hammer
1935	Clacton Entertainers of 1935	Jack Richards	Will Hammer
1936	West End Vanities	Tubby Harold	Will Hammer
1937	Revelry at the West Cliff	Fred Gibson	Will Hammer
1938	Vaudeville at the West Cliff	Jack Rowlands	Will Hammer
1939	Swingtime at the West Cliff	Henry Arges	Will Hammer
1940-1945 No Show			
1946	Victory Vanities	Will Hammer, Ivy Luck	Will Hammer
1947	For the Fun of it	Nosmo King, Frankie Howerd	Will Hammer
1948	For the Fun of it	Alec Pleon	Will Hammer
1949	Sunshine & Smiles	Bunny Baron, Ivy Luck	Will Hammer
1950	Sunshine & Smiles	Bunny Baron, Ivy Luck	Will Hammer
1951	Sunshine & Smiles	Bennett & Williams	Jack Payne & Will Hammer
1952	Holiday Fanfare	Charles Harrison	Jack Payne & Will Hammer
1953	Come to the Show	Jack Francois	Renee Paskin and Will Hammer
1954	Come to the Show	Jack Francois	Renee Paskin and Will Hammer
1955	Joy Bells	Joe Black	Will Hammer and Mildred Challenger
1956	Joy Bells	Joe Black	Will Hammer and Mildred Challenger
1957	Fine & Dandy	Kenneth Earle and Malcolm Vaughan	Will Hammer and Neville Kennard
1958	The Rayker Revue	Gordon Needham	Raymond Kerry
1959	No show		
1960	Penguin Players Repertory Season	The Penguin Players with Rex Deering	Richard Burnett
1961	Penguin Players	The Penguin Players with Rex Deering	The Penguin Players
1962	Galleon Theatre Company	The Galleon Theatre Company with Clyde Pollitt	Derek Pollitt
1963	Galleon Theatre Company	The Galleon Theatre Company with Clyde Pollitt	The Galleon Theatre Company
1964	Galleon Players	The Galleon Theatre Company with Clyde Pollitt	The Galleon Theatre Company